HUMVEES

John Willis

www.av2books.com

AV² provides enriched content that supplements and complements this book. Weigl's AV² books strive to create inspired learning and engage young minds in a total learning experience.

Your AV² Media Enhanced books come alive with...

 **Audio**
Listen to sections of the book read aloud.

 **Video**
Watch informative video clips.

 **Embedded Weblinks**
Gain additional information for research.

 **Try This!**
Complete activities and hands-on experiments.

 **Key Words**
Study vocabulary, and complete a matching word activity.

 **Quizzes**
Test your knowledge.

 **Slide Show**
View images and captions, and prepare a presentation.

... and much, much more!

Go to www.av2books.com, and enter this book's unique code.

BOOK CODE

T956937

AV² by Weigl brings you media enhanced books that support active learning.

Published by AV² by Weigl
350 5th Avenue, 59th Floor New York, NY 10118
Website: www.av2books.com

Copyright ©2017 AV² by Weigl
All rights reserved. No part of this publication may be reproduced, stored in a retrieval system, or transmitted in any form or by any means, electronic, mechanical, photocopying, recording, or otherwise, without the prior written permission of the publisher.

Library of Congress Cataloging-in-Publication Data

Names: Willis, John, 1989- author.
Title: Humvees / John Willis.
Description: New York, NY : Weigl, [2017] | Series: Mighty military machines
 | Includes index.
Identifiers: LCCN 2016034501 (print) | LCCN 2016034570 (ebook) | ISBN
 9781489647658 (hard cover : alk. paper) | ISBN 9781489650863 (soft cover :
 alk. paper) | ISBN 9781489647665 (Multi-user ebk.)
Subjects: LCSH: Hummer trucks--Juvenile literature.
Classification: LCC UG618 .W5 2017 (print) | LCC UG618 (ebook) | DDC
 623.74/722--dc23
LC record available at https://lccn.loc.gov/2016034501

Printed in the United States of America in Brainerd, Minnesota
1 2 3 4 5 6 7 8 9 0 20 19 18 17 16

082016   Editor: Katie Gillespie
210716   Art Director: Terry Paulhus

Weigl acknowledges Getty Images and Alamy as the primary image suppliers for this title.

HUMVEES

CONTENTS

- 2 AV² Book Code
- 4 What Are Humvees?
- 6 Kinds of Humvees
- 8 Heavy Humvees
- 10 Humvee Tires
- 12 Transporting Humvees
- 14 First Humvees
- 16 Future Transports
- 18 Civilian Use
- 20 Staying Safe
- 22 Humvee Facts
- 24 Key Words

Humvees are vehicles with four wheels and a wide body. They are used by the United States military.

There are 15 different kinds of Humvee. Some Humvees carry cargo. Others are used to move soldiers.

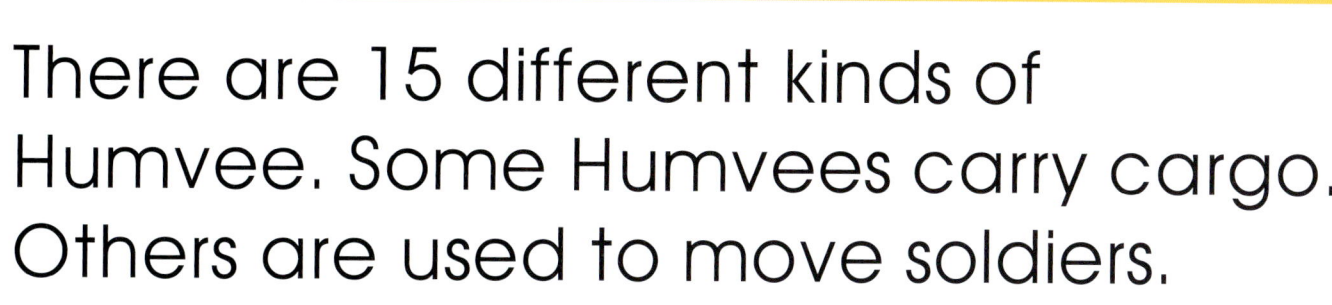

More than 280,000 Humvees have been made for military use.

A Humvee can weigh more than a rhinoceros. Humvees are made of aluminum to keep their weight down.

Although they are heavy, Humvees can move faster than a cheetah.

The driver can change the amount of air in the tires from inside the Humvee. This lets it drive over different kinds of ground.

A Humvee's large tires keep its body up high so it can drive over objects in its path.

Humvees can be flown around the world in airplanes. This lets them reach places where they are needed.

Humvees can be dropped out of airplanes using parachutes.

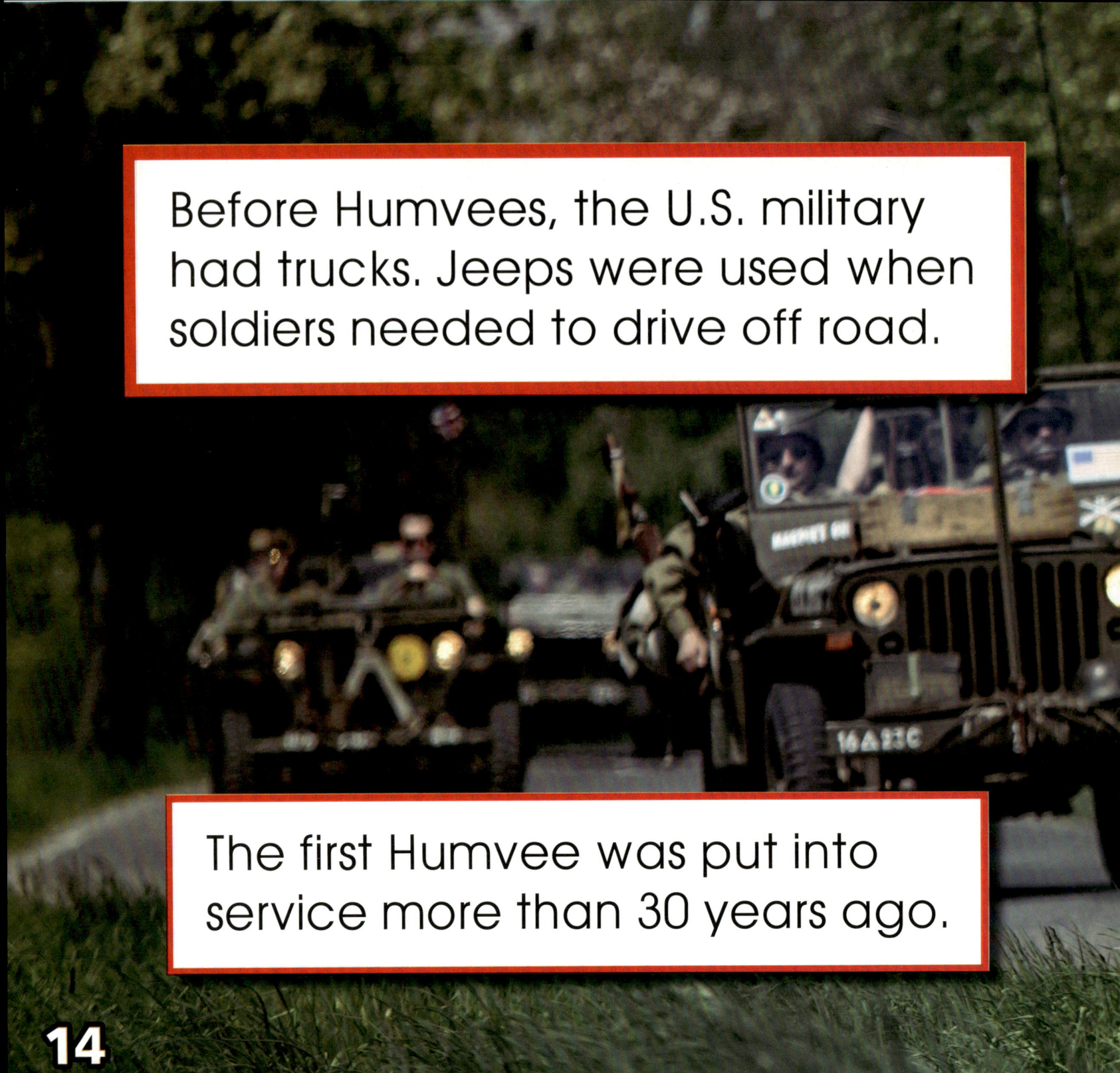

Before Humvees, the U.S. military had trucks. Jeeps were used when soldiers needed to drive off road.

The first Humvee was put into service more than 30 years ago.

The Joint Light Tactical Vehicle (JLTV) will replace the Humvee in 2018. It can travel over difficult ground like a Humvee and has armor like a tank.

The JLTV can drive through water up to 5 feet deep.

People who are not in the military are called civilians. The civilian version of the Humvee is called a Hummer.

Like the Humvee, a Hummer is able to drive off road.

Riding in a Humvee can be dangerous. Humvees have special features to keep the driver and passengers safe.

HUMVEE FACTS

These pages provide more detail about the interesting facts found in the book. They are intended to be used by adults as a learning support to help young readers round out their knowledge of each machine featured in the *Mighty Military Machines* series.

Pages 4–5

Humvees are vehicles with four wheels and a wide body. Their full name is High Mobility Multi-purpose Wheeled Vehicle (HMMWV). Humvees are 6 feet (1.8 meters) tall, but 7 feet (2.1 m) wide. These proportions give stability, making Humvees difficult to tip over. They are currently used by all branches of the United States military.

Pages 6–7

There are 15 different kinds of Humvee. While there are many configurations, all Humvees share common features, such as the engine and chassis. Many Humvees are used as transports or ambulances. Others fulfill combat roles. Specialized Humvees can carry tube-launched, optically-tracked, wireless-guided (TOW) missiles for anti-armor roles, or Stinger missiles to defend against aerial attacks.

Pages 8–9

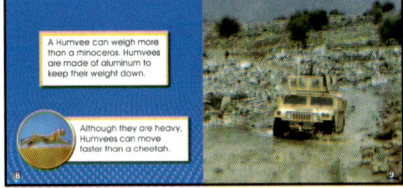

A Humvee can weigh more than a rhinoceros. The choice of aluminum as a building material provides several advantages. In addition to reducing the overall weight of the Humvee, aluminum provides the vehicle with rust resistance. The panels that make up the body are designed to flex when traveling over difficult terrain.

Pages 10–11

The driver can change the amount of air in the tires from inside the Humvee. Independent suspension and four-wheel drive allow travel over a wide range of terrain, including steep slopes, and up to 60 inches (152 centimeters) of water. A Humvee's body is kept about 16 inches (41 cm) off the ground while carrying a typically sized load. A diesel engine lets it reach speeds of 70 miles (113 kilometers) per hour.

Pages 12–13

Humvees can be flown around the world in airplanes. Depending on the transport aircraft, up to 15 Humvees can be flown by air in a single airplane. By using the Low-Altitude Parachute Extraction System (LAPES), they can be dropped by air.

Pages 14–15

Before Humvees, the U.S. military had trucks. Prior to the Humvee, the M151 Jeep was the standard U.S. military transport vehicle. While it possessed independent suspension, it often rolled when turning at high speeds. The military started searching for a replacement in the late 1970s, and officially chose the Humvee in 1983. Humvees first saw combat during Operation Just Cause in 1989.

Pages 16–17

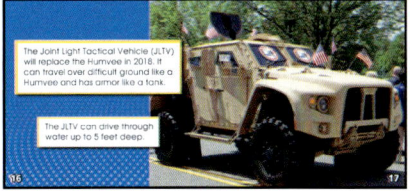

The Joint Light Tactical Vehicle (JLTV) will replace the Humvee in 2018. Although Humvees are designed for serviceability, the military has been considering several replacement options. The winning design, Oshkosh's Light Combat Tactical All-Terrain Vehicle (L-ATV), outperforms the current Humvees in the field. Features include 20 inches (51 cm) of ground clearance, a hybrid electric-diesel engine, and advanced blast armor.

Pages 18–19

People who are not in the military are called civilians. The first civilian Humvee, or Hummer, went on sale in 1992. Although inefficient and heavy, it became popular due to its high safety scores and durability. In 2005, the lighter-weight H3 model entered the market, and production of the original Hummer ceased the following year. The H3 was designed to weigh less and use fuel more efficiently than earlier Hummers.

Pages 20–21

Riding in a Humvee can be dangerous. Some Humvees have armored glass windows and a steel crew area. When first tested, Humvees were twice as sturdy as required by the military. Upgraded models such as the M1151A1 include shielded gunnery positions, and improvised explosive device (IED) countermeasures. Increased armor also provides protection against small arms fire.

KEY WORDS

Research has shown that as much as 65 percent of all written material published in English is made up of 300 words. These 300 words cannot be taught using pictures or learned by sounding them out. They must be recognized by sight. This book contains 68 common sight words to help young readers improve their reading fluency and comprehension. This book also teaches young readers several important content words, such as proper nouns. These words are paired with pictures to aid in learning and improve understanding.

Page	Sight Words First Appearance
4	a, and, are, by, four, the, they, used, with
7	been, carry, different, for, have, kinds, made, more, move, of, others, some, than, there, to
8	can, down, keep, their
11	air, change, from, high, in, it, its, large, lets, over, so, this, up
12	around, be, out, places, them, where, world
14	before, first, had, into, off, put, was, were, when, years
16	feet, has, like, through, water, will
19	is, not, people, who

Page	Content Words First Appearance
4	body, Humvees, military, vehicles, wheels
7	cargo, soldiers
8	aluminum, cheetah, rhinoceros, weight
11	amount, driver, ground, inside, objects, path, tires
12	airplanes, parachutes
14	Jeeps, road, service, trucks
16	armor, Joint Light Tactical Vehicle, tank
19	civilians, Hummer, version
20	features, passengers

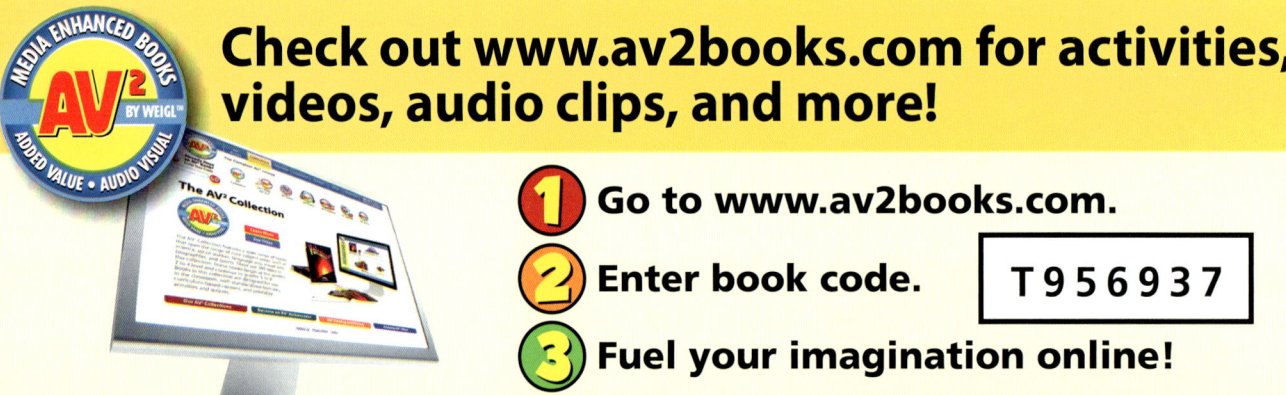

Check out www.av2books.com for activities, videos, audio clips, and more!

1. Go to www.av2books.com.
2. Enter book code. T956937
3. Fuel your imagination online!

www.av2books.com